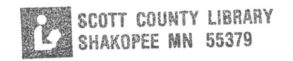

HOW PAPER IS MADE

I WONDER
HOW PAPER IS MADE

Neil Curtis and Peter Greenland

Lerner Publications Company • Minneapolis

This edition published 1992
by Lerner Publications Company
241 First Avenue North
Minneapolis, Minnesota 55401 USA

Original edition published in 1990 by Heinemann Educational Books
Ltd., Halley Court, Jordan Hill, Oxford OX28EJ England
Copyright © 1990 by Heinemann Educational Books Ltd.

Library of Congress Cataloging-in-Publication Data

Curtis, Neil.
  How paper is made / Neil Curtis and Peter Greenland.
    p.   cm. — (I wonder)
  Originally published: Oxford, England : Heinemann
Educational Books, 1990.
  Summary: Describes how paper is made, beginning in a
forest and ending in a paper mill.
  ISBN 0-8225-2376-0
  1. Papermaking—Juvenile literature. [1. Papermaking.]
I. Greenland, Peter. II. Title. III. Series: Curtis, Neil. I wonder.
TS1105.5.C87   1992
676'.2—dc20   91-23453
                                                        CIP
                                                        AC

Manufactured in the United States of America.

1 2 3 4 5 6 7 8 9 10 01 00 99 98 97 96 95 94 93 92

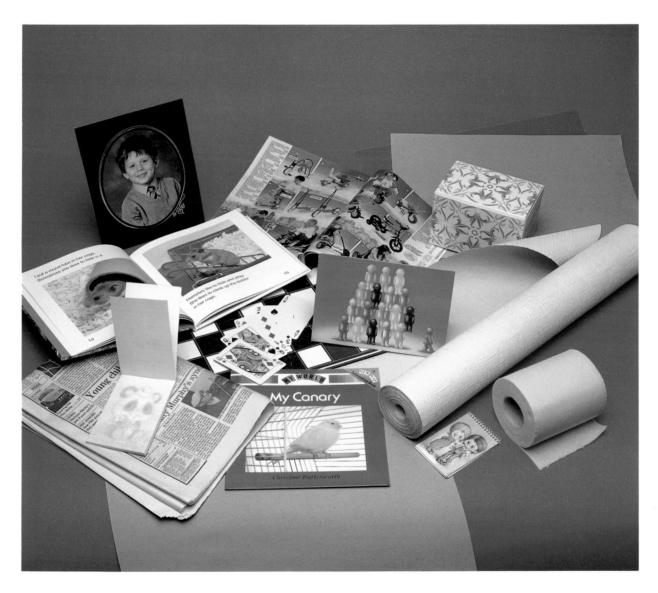

Paper is used to make many things.
Books, magazines, and cards are made from paper.

Most paper is made from wood.
Some trees are planted
just for making paper.

Forestry workers cut down the trees.
They cut the trunks of the trees into logs.
Then cranes load the logs onto trucks.

The logs are taken to a paper mill.
There, another crane unloads the logs.

The mill stores the logs in a big yard.
Workers spray the logs with water
to keep them from drying out.

Inside the paper mill, power saws cut the logs into smaller pieces.

Bark is not used to make paper.
It is stripped from the wood.

Then the wood goes into a machine
where it is ground and crushed.

A liquid comes out of the machine.
The liquid is called pulp.

Pulp can also be made from waste paper.
Using waste paper to make pulp
is called recycling.

The pulp flows through a pipe
into another giant machine.

The wet pulp flows onto a plastic or wire mesh.
The mesh shakes from side to side
to spread the pulp evenly.

A sheet of damp paper is formed.

Heavy rollers squeeze the water out.
Then the paper goes over heated rollers that dry it.

A special coating is added to the paper.
The coating will make words and pictures
printed on the paper look very clear.

Workers check the paper, using computers.
They measure how thick the paper is
and make sure that it is dry.

Finished paper is rolled onto giant reels.

The paper mill is very noisy.

Workers must wear ear protection at all times.

Overhead cranes carry the rolls of coated paper
to the other end of the factory.
There the paper will be cut.

The giant roll of paper is cut into shorter rolls.
A worker tapes down the end of each roll
to keep it from unwinding.

A machine wraps the rolls in brown paper.

The rolls of paper are stored in a warehouse.
Printers will buy the paper to make magazines and
books just like this one.